קִדּוּשׁ

Do you remember that the קִדּוּשׁ is one of the בְּרָכוֹת we say to welcome and sanctify Shabbat? We also say it on many holidays, including Rosh Hashanah, Sukkot, and Pesaḥ. The קִדּוּשׁ separates these occasions from the everyday and helps us to make them holy.

The קִדּוּשׁ begins with the blessing over the wine, thanking God for creating the fruit of the vine—the grapes from which we make wine.

The קִדּוּשׁ for Shabbat reminds us that we were chosen by God with love to observe Shabbat and to carry out God's commandments.

The קִדּוּשׁ begins with a בְּרָכָה you have already learned.

בָּרוּךְ אַתָּה, יְיָ אֱלֹהֵינוּ, מֶלֶךְ הָעוֹלָם, בּוֹרֵא פְּרִי הַגָּפֶן.

Can you say this בְּרָכָה by heart?

Practice reading the קִדּוּשׁ for Shabbat aloud.

1. בָּרוּךְ אַתָּה, יְיָ אֱלֹהֵינוּ, מֶלֶךְ הָעוֹלָם, בּוֹרֵא פְּרִי הַגָּפֶן.
2. בָּרוּךְ אַתָּה, יְיָ אֱלֹהֵינוּ, מֶלֶךְ הָעוֹלָם, אֲשֶׁר קִדְּשָׁנוּ
3. בְּמִצְוֹתָיו וְרָצָה בָנוּ, וְשַׁבַּת קָדְשׁוֹ בְּאַהֲבָה וּבְרָצוֹן
4. הִנְחִילָנוּ, זִכָּרוֹן לְמַעֲשֵׂה בְרֵאשִׁית. כִּי הוּא יוֹם תְּחִלָּה
5. לְמִקְרָאֵי קֹדֶשׁ, זֵכֶר לִיצִיאַת מִצְרָיִם. כִּי בָנוּ בָחַרְתָּ
6. וְאוֹתָנוּ קִדַּשְׁתָּ מִכָּל הָעַמִּים, וְשַׁבַּת קָדְשְׁךָ בְּאַהֲבָה
7. וּבְרָצוֹן הִנְחַלְתָּנוּ. בָּרוּךְ אַתָּה יְיָ, מְקַדֵּשׁ הַשַּׁבָּת.

Praised are You, Adonai our God, Ruler of the world, who creates the fruit of the vine.
Praised are You, Adonai our God, Ruler of the world, who makes us holy
with commandments and takes delight in us. In God's love and favor God has made the
holy Sabbath our heritage, as a memory of the work of creation.
It is first among our holy days, a memory of the going out from Egypt.
You chose us from all the nations and You made us holy, and in (with) love and favor You
have given us the Sabbath as a sacred inheritance.
Praised are You, Adonai, who makes the Sabbath holy.

PRAYER DICTIONARY

קִדּוּשׁ
sanctification

זִכָּרוֹן
memory

(לְ)מַעֲשֵׂה בְּרֵאשִׁית
work of creation

זֵכֶר
memory

(לְ)יְצִיאַת מִצְרַיִם
going out from Egypt

בְּאַהֲבָה
in (with) love

וּבְרָצוֹן
and in (with) favor

WORD CHECK

Put a ✔ next to the Hebrew word that means the same as the English.

.ı memory   ☐ אַהֲבָה
  ☐ זִכָּרוֹן

.2 and in (with) favor   ☐ וּבְרָצוֹן
  ☐ וְרָצָה

.3 memory   ☐ זֵכֶר
  ☐ מִצְרַיִם

.4 sanctification   ☐ קִדּוּשׁ
  ☐ בָּרוּךְ

.5 work of creation   ☐ נֵר שֶׁל שַׁבָּת
  ☐ מַעֲשֵׂה בְּרֵאשִׁית

.6 in (with) love   ☐ בְּאַהֲבָה
  ☐ בְּרֵאשִׁית

.7 going out from Egypt   ☐ לְעוֹלָם וָעֶד
  ☐ יְצִיאַת מִצְרַיִם

2

Prayer Building Blocks

קִדּוּשׁ "sanctification"

We know that the root letters קדשׁ mean "holy."

קִדּוּשׁ means "sanctification"
(the act of making something holy)

קִדּוּשׁ helps make שַׁבָּת holy.

The following words all appear in the Kiddush.

Circle the three root letters in each word. Read the words aloud.

מְקַדֵּשׁ קָדְשְׁךָ קִדַּשְׁתָּ קֹדֶשׁ קָדְשׁוֹ קִדְּשָׁנוּ

Read the following lines, and circle the words built on the root קדשׁ.

1. וְשַׁבַּת קָדְשׁוֹ בְּאַהֲבָה וּבְרָצוֹן הִנְחִילָנוּ
2. נְקַדֵּשׁ אֶת שִׁמְךָ בָּעוֹלָם כְּשֵׁם שֶׁמַּקְדִּישִׁים אוֹתוֹ
3. וַיְבָרֶךְ אֱלֹהִים אֶת יוֹם הַשְּׁבִיעִי וַיְקַדֵּשׁ אֹתוֹ
4. קָדוֹשׁ קָדוֹשׁ קָדוֹשׁ יְיָ צְבָאוֹת
5. אַתָּה קִדַּשְׁתָּ אֶת יוֹם הַשְּׁבִיעִי לִשְׁמֶךָ

Put a ✔ next to the ways we can add holiness to our lives.

____ lighting Shabbat candles   ____ watching television

____ watching a golden sunset   ____ baking brownies for a sick friend

____ studying the Torah   ____ going to the mall

Can you add one more example of your own?

_____

IMAGINE THAT

The reason the קִדּוּשׁ begins with a blessing over wine may be because in olden times, the drinking of wine was thought of as regal or royal. Starting with this taste of royalty adds a touch of even greater honor and specialness to our celebration.

The cup of wine used for Kiddush is usually filled right to the top. This is to show that our happiness is brimming over as we bless יְיָ. We hope that our lives will overflow with good things.

Think About This!

The Jews are members of a "holy nation." Each and every one of us has the potential to be holy. Fulfilling mitzvot can add holiness to our lives. What do you think "being holy" means?

Prayer Building Blocks

זִכָּרוֹן, זֵכֶר   "memory," "remembrance"

The קִדּוּשׁ recited on שַׁבָּת helps us *remember* why we celebrate שַׁבָּת and make it holy.

The letters זכר tell us that "remember" is part of a word's meaning.

זִכָּרוֹן   means "memory" or "remembrance."

זֵכֶר   also means "memory" or "remembrance."

What three letters are in both זֵכֶר and זִכָּרוֹן? ___ ___ ___

The קִדּוּשׁ helps us remember events in our history that are reasons for joy. One reason for joy is mentioned in these words from the קִדּוּשׁ.

זִכָּרוֹן לְמַעֲשֵׂה בְרֵאשִׁית

remembrance of the work of creation

Circle the Hebrew word that means "memory" or "remembrance."

....

Another reason for joy is found in the following words from the קִדּוּשׁ prayer.

זֵכֶר לִיצִיאַת מִצְרָיִם

memory of the going out from Egypt

Circle the Hebrew word that means "memory" or "remembrance."

....

Which three letters tell us that "remember" is part of a word's meaning?

____   ____   ____

Read the following sentences and circle the words built on the root זכר.

1. וַיֹּאמֶר מֹשֶׁה אֶל הָעָם, זָכוֹר אֶת הַיּוֹם הַזֶּה.

2. בָּרוּךְ אַתָּה, יְיָ אֱלֹהֵינוּ, מֶלֶךְ הָעוֹלָם, זוֹכֵר הַבְּרִית, וְנֶאֱמָן בִּבְרִיתוֹ וְקַיָּם בְּמַאֲמָרוֹ.

3. מְקַדֵּשׁ יִשְׂרָאֵל וְיוֹם הַזִּכָּרוֹן.

4. לְמַעַן תִּזְכְּרוּ וַעֲשִׂיתֶם אֶת כָּל מִצְוֹתָי, וִהְיִיתֶם קְדֹשִׁים לֵאלֹהֵיכֶם.

5. וּזְכַרְתֶּם אֶת כָּל מִצְוֹת יְיָ וַעֲשִׂיתֶם אֹתָם.

Prayer Building Blocks

(לְ)מַעֲשֵׂה בְּרֵאשִׁית "work of creation"

When we say קָדוֹשׁ we remember two important events. One of them is the creation of the world.

מַעֲשֵׂה means "work of."

בְּרֵאשִׁית means "creation" (in the beginning).

בְּרֵאשִׁית is also the Hebrew name for Genesis, the first book of the תּוֹרָה.

Which of the following is not a meaning of בְּרֵאשִׁית? Circle it.

creation   Torah   Genesis   in the beginning

Draw a circle around the Hebrew word that means "the work of."

זִכָּרוֹן לְמַעֲשֵׂה בְּרֵאשִׁית

Now draw a star above the Hebrew word that means "creation."

(לְ)יְצִיאַת מִצְרָיִם "going out from Egypt"

The second important event we remember in the קָדוֹשׁ is the *going out from Egypt*.

יְצִיאַת means "going out from."

מִצְרָיִם means "Egypt."

Draw a circle around the Hebrew word that means "going out from."

זֶכֶר לִיצִיאַת מִצְרָיִם

Now draw a star above the Hebrew word that means "Egypt."

בְּאַהֲבָה "in (with) love"

בְּאַהֲבָה   means "in (with) love."

בְּאַהֲבָה   is made up of two parts:

בְּ   at the beginning of a word means "in" or "with."

אַהֲבָה   means "love."

Circle the prefix that means "in" or "with" in the following Hebrew word.

בְּאַהֲבָה

To the following prefix, add the Hebrew word meaning "love."

_____ בְּ

וּבְרָצוֹן "and in (with) favor"

וּבְרָצוֹן   means "and in (with) favor."

וּבְרָצוֹן   is made up of three parts:

וּ   means "and."

בְּ   at the beginning of a word means "in" or "with."

רָצוֹן   means "favor."

Circle the prefix that means "and" in the following Hebrew word.

וּבְרָצוֹן

To the following prefixes, add the Hebrew word meaning "favor."

_____ וּבְ

FLUENT READING

Practice reading the lines below.

1. וַיְכֻלּוּ הַשָּׁמַיִם וְהָאָרֶץ וְכָל צְבָאָם.

2. וַיְבָרֶךְ אֱלֹהִים אֶת יוֹם הַשְּׁבִיעִי וַיְקַדֵּשׁ אֹתוֹ.

3. וּמֵבִיא גוֹאֵל לִבְנֵי בְנֵיהֶם, לְמַעַן שְׁמוֹ, בְּאַהֲבָה.

4. עֲבָדִים הָיִינוּ לְפַרְעֹה בְּמִצְרָיִם.

5. אַתָּה קִדַּשְׁתָּ אֶת יוֹם הַשְּׁבִיעִי לִשְׁמֶךָ.

6. לִבְנֵי יִשְׂרָאֵל עַם קְרֹבוֹ, הַלְלוּיָהּ!

7. זָכוֹר אֶת יוֹם הַשַּׁבָּת לְקַדְּשׁוֹ.

8. אִלּוּ הוֹצִיאָנוּ מִמִּצְרַיִם וְלֹא קָרַע לָנוּ אֶת הַיָּם – דַּיֵּנוּ!

9. בָּרוּךְ אַתָּה, יְיָ אֱלֹהֵינוּ, מֶלֶךְ הָעוֹלָם, אֲשֶׁר בָּחַר בָּנוּ מִכָּל הָעַמִּים וְנָתַן לָנוּ אֶת תּוֹרָתוֹ.

ISBN 978-0-87441-752-4